GHOSTS OF PAST AND FUTURE

BORGO PRESS BOOKS BY DARRELL SCHWEITZER:

Conan's World and Robert E. Howard
Exploring Fantasy Worlds
The Fantastic Horizon
Ghosts of Past and Future: Selected Poetry
Speaking of Horror II

GHOSTS OF PAST AND FUTURE

SELECTED POETRY

by

Darrell Schweitzer

The Borgo Press
An Imprint of Wildside Press LLC

MMVIII

Borgo Laureate Series
ISSN 1082-3336

Number Three

Printed in the United States of America

www.wildsidepress.com

FIRST EDITION

CONTENTS

PART ONE: INTIMATIONS BEYOND MORTALITY

PART TWO: THE MATTER OF BRITAIN

PART THREE: POST-HOMERICA

PART FOUR: YESTERDAY'S TOMORROWS

To the Memory of

Joseph Lalli

PART ONE

INTIMATIONS BEYOND MORTALITY

DENYING GHOSTS

I do not think that I shall rise
out of my grave each night
and drift like patchy fog
through all those familiar places
now known, without any irony,
as my old haunts;
nor do my future plans include
moaning and shrieking and rattling chains,
or ingratiating myself like a chilly wind
into a former lover's bed
to whisper of secret sins;
and I certainly have no intention
of being conjured by masters of forbidden lore
to utter ghastly, cosmic dooms,
and topple kings from off their thrones
or the gods from out of heaven.

I neither fear these things,
nor expect them.
I only fear those still alive
who do expect them.

Cemetery Tour, Montréal, Early November 2001

So we made our little jokes
and took our pictures
in the rain and the gathering dark,
as the mausoleums,
like cramped, windowless houses,
stood in sullen silhouette
against the yellow leaves
and the orange glow of the city sky.

Maybe we grew a little less jolly
with the realization that there was real pain here,
that the ones who passed through these iron doors,
into these narrow houses, were still loved,
and even the pink lawn flamingos on one of the graves
didn't seem as funny anymore,
as the dead waited patiently
for us to leave.

DEATH IS THE GREAT UNWINDING

Death is the great unwinding,
like a ball of string undone.
The relatives slip away from your grave
by ones and twos,
the sun breaks through the clouds,
and after a while you get up,
touch your wife's hand again,
and promise to love her forever.
Then you return your gold watch to the office,
and sit down at your desk,
full of the experience and wisdom
of so many years on the job,
and take up your labors with real fervor,
forgetting everything as you blunder your way
down the corporate ladder
until they finally show you the door.
For the moment you are free as air,
the world is your oyster,
and the one you'd sworn to love,
is just a name among many,
until the school bell rings,
and unwillingly you drag yourself inside,

to forget so many lessons,
in favor of cartoon shows
and games of shoot-the-man-down,
and getting your bottom paddled
for unremembered transgressions
that seemed so right at the time.
But even parental pig-headedness fades,
and you unremember in flashes now:
going into the darkened attic alone during a thunderstorm,
the musty, waxen smell of great-grandmother,
when you were raised in her arms for a kiss,
and dumping a bowl of applesauce on your head
because you just had to do it,
and some impossible-to-retrieve dream
about boys in pajamas, running,
who had once been Indians with Peter Pan.
Then life doesn't come reeling back like a yo-yo.
There's nothing on the end of the string.
That's it, then.
That.

We Dead Outnumber the Living, You Know

We dead outnumber the living, you know.
For all you desperately try to outbreed us,
the fruits of your loins inevitably
switch sides in the end.
Back in the Ages of Faith,
you efficiently shuffled us off
to Heaven or to Hell,
and only the infrequent ghost lingered,
to be speedily dealt with
by formalities read out of books.
But *now* we're like bubbles in a broth
brought furiously to boil.
Now is the time for the breaking of graves,
the air filled with unpardonable stench,
Jack Death nipping at your nose,
and zombies, zombies everywhere,
this overpopulation of corpses
the inescapable reminder
of what you are to become.
Won't that be fun?
Won't that be fun?

No, I do not think it will be fun,
as the terror becomes absolute
and settles into monotonous despair,
all of us groping uselessly for the lost door
to Heaven, or even to Hell.
No, I don't think it will be fun.

I MISS THE NIGHT SKY

I miss the night sy.
        In the city,
you can't see much:
only the moon
and the very brightest stars;
the glorious Milky Way remains
unsuspected, unimagined
by most who live out their lives
within the city's glare.

I miss the night sky.
        In the grave,
the stars of the deathlands,
are few and faint and strange,
the last fading embers
of fires already extinguished,
and we who rise up out of the grave
are too preoccupied with our pain
to pause and look at the night sky.

Look How the Moonlight Makes Us Young Again

Look how the moonlight makes us young again.
We who have loved for so long
now lie among the marble of these tombs,
caressing with cold hands,
bathed in that perfect light,
ourselves made perfect once more,
gleaming, smooth, as exquisite
as newly polished stone.
Look how the moonlight makes us young again!

THOSE WHO DO NOT FIND THEIR WAY INTO ELFLAND

Black Jack Davey danced into the gloaming;
Tam Lin fell from his horse in the darkening wood;
King Orfeo played his harp before a long, gray stone;
Tom O'Bedlam was there all along;
and True Thomas, most famous of them all,
waited beneath a tree until
the Fairy Queen herself
took him on her milk-white steed,
for forty days and forty nights,
riding in red blood to the knee.

But those who would command
the wonder to appear,
can pore over their maps,
blow their horns,
and gallop till they drop,
and what they will experience after that
will be, no doubt, only delirium.

The dream comes as the dream comes.
Seek it without seeking,

as True Thomas did, sitting still.
If you reach out and try to grab it,
Elfland will recede from you,
as the tide over flat sand,
across a space that would weary the comet.

The Unmapped Shore

There are no waves upon that sea
that stretches to the unmapped shore
beneath the faint, uncharted stars.

We pile into our gaudy barge
silks and jewels, golden masks,
and records of our earthly deeds,
tablets fulsome with self-praise,
addressed, by guile, to silent gods.

Yet the purpose of these things
is not to ease or speed the trip,
but to delay or to defer
by ballast's weight, by sail raised up
to catch some wild, rebellious wind.

But no wind rises on that sea.
The steady current bears us on
to the dark and unmapped shore.

DREADS

What if our wizards are long-winded frauds,
and poor Tom's just left a'cold,
and what if our specters are shadows and wind,
and half-garbled memories grown old?
And what, too, if there aren't any dragons,
nor gods on Olympus, nor ogre nor elf,
and a knight's quest ends with a Triple-A map,
and the Grail gathers dust on a shelf?

I say that we *need* our shambling beasts,
zombies and hundred-foot apes,
and tentacled things from out of the deep,
and vampires in dark opera capes.
How much braver to conquer them, then,
creating ourselves what we fear.
The point is not tilting at windmills,
but making the giants appear.

WHY THERE ARE GHOSTS

The boast, the curse,
the desperately unfunny joke,
words, once spoken,
which can never be called back:
that's why there are ghosts.

The gentle touch, the whisper,
that might have changed
the destinies of lives,
the unopened door:
that's why there are ghosts.

When you return, all grown up,
to that secret place in the woods,
and find it all wrong, shrunken,
unremarkable in the all-revealing light:
that's why there are ghosts.

WITCHES IN WINTER

Those aren't crows,
the tiny specks that you see
just above the horizon,
against the steely sky,
as the night comes on
and the dead cornstalks
rattle in the frigid wind.

Those aren't crows,
screeching, faint and far away,
as cattle die amid the barren fields,
and old people shiver by the fire,
certain they'll never see the spring,
as sick children cry out in delirium,
and shadows deepen and nightmares begin.

Those aren't crows.

THOMAS THE RHYMER RETURNS TO ELFLAND

This much is known and written
and probably true, that when
his days on Earth were done,
there came before True Thomas,
the prophet who could not lie,
the poet who had seen
more beauty than is in the world,
a white hart and a white hind,
which no blade might harm,
nor any hunter slay, and he,
knowing what they were,
rose at once from his feasting,
bade farewell to his kinsmen,
and followed the miraculous beasts
into the cold and gathering dark.

But it is not written, nor well known,
that the Queen of Elfland came to him
in that gathering dark, and took him up
onto her horse again, riding
into a hill and under a stone,

knee-deep in the blood of all the world's slain,
becoming a loathly hag again,
a thing of charnel tatters,
until she reached the further shore,
where her beauty was multiplied ten thousand-fold,
and True Thomas gave himself over,
one last time, with a kiss,
beholding as he had before,
the splendid colors of Elfland,
which are not in the world.

But in an instant,
all the colors faded,
even as the gold of Elfland
dissolves into brown leaves,
even as the fruits of that country
do not nourish and its wine
has the taste of frigid, wintry air;
for he was a dead man now,
who knew not whether Heaven or Hell
had granted this boon,
that he should journey to neither place
but reside in Elfland, beside his Queen,
forever.
"It is enough," she said,
and the voice of his reply
was as the wind,
whispering in her ear,
and stirring the grey dust
at her feet.
"Enough."

THE SPIRIT THAT FLED FROM JULIAN'S TENT (A.D. 363)

The spirit that fled from Julian's tent was,
we are told, dark and utterly silent,
like a shadow, or a tent flap stirring in the desert breeze,
though witnesses swear there was no wind that night.
Who can say? Attention was obviously directed elsewhere,
to the emperor, loquaciously dying, trying to play Socrates
as he had played Alexander, theatrical to the last,
discoursing on the nature of the soul, even as he lay
with a Persian spear in his side. (But was it a Persian
spear, or a Roman one? Who can be sure?)
We do know that when the physician drew the spearhead
out,
a piece of intestine came away on the barbed point,
the wound bled copiously, and Julian asked for water,
then expired, having forgotten in the press of the moment
to utter the kind of last words a historian
would have to supply for him later.
It must have been just then
that somebody turned away, out of disgust or modesty,
and glimpsed, leaving the tent, the apparition,

shade, divine guardian, imperial genius,
or whatever it was, its pale, round face
when it glanced back one last time,
as startling as an unexpected moon.
Later elaboration has it walking
(though its feet never touched the ground)
with greatest dignity across the desert floor,
its black cloak billowing fantastically (although there
was no wind), not in flight, but with deliberation,
like an ambassador whose mission is over,
returning to his own country.
The thing must have passed through the Persian lines,
for the enemy, like wolves sensing a kill,
had gathered close, but no Persian source
mentions anything of the sort.
A mystery then, and the rest is history,
which tells us merely that the spirit left,
and Julian, dying, did not curse his gods,
who had played him false and left him to perish,
whether nobly or not, they did not care,
in the windless night.

EDGAR ALLAN POE NEARS HIS END

He was doomed by 1847,
with Virginia gone, transformed
by disease into an exquisite china doll.
Now art and life commingled,
as he crept out silently,
secretly, to mourn his Annabel Lee
in her chilly tomb.
Oh, he put up a brave front,
a pretense of returning to life,
as he received guests courteously,
and even outclassed several gentlemen
in the boyish spectacle of a jumping contest
in which he split his gaiters.

But those who diagnosed "brain fever,"
drawing on whatever quackeries or ill-wishes,
more or less had it right:
he was not long for this world,
for all his seeming vigor,
the resumption of literary slugfests,
and even his frantic, preposterous
outpourings of love to Annie Richmond,

Sarah Helen Whitman, and others,
as if he might actually find
in a *living* woman, the Ideal he sought.
These things were masks, which had to come off,
as the festival ended, as inexorably he voyaged,
like the traveler gliding into Arnheim
(by way of Auber, Weir, and Usher),
toward the cataract, and the towering, shrouded
figure that Arthur Gordon Pym saw,
whose hue was of the perfect whiteness of snow.
There. *There.* In the abyss.
The impossible Mystery, the Hieroglyph.
His pain was unbearable then.

I KNOW IT'S TIME TO DANCE WITH DEATH

I know it's time to dance with Death
when all the wines are flat,
when all the songs now sound as one,
and wisdom seems but noise.
In swirling waltz, in graceful step,
I dance with Death at last,
her face a ghostly, risen moon,
her dark eyes hard as glass.
But when I lean to kiss her mouth,
she fades before the sun,
and all the songs still sound the same,
and all the wines are flat.

Old Friends

We dead leave no footprints in the snow,
and when we summon you to the door,
you say it's the wind, or rustling ivy,
or a dry branch scraping a window pane.

We wait voiceless in the dark,
in our hunger and our rage,
for you to wander out that door,
or lean out the window into the night.

For we are your ineradicable past
and your inescapable future.

The Colossi of Memnon Near Thebes (Second or Third Century A.D.)

Sometimes, on moonless nights,
when only the brilliant stars
gleam on the black Nile;
with the desert wind at their backs,
the great statues are heard to converse:

"I remember playing by the river's edge.
The mud was soft between my toes.
Women scolded me.
I was terribly afraid of crocodiles."

"I am a god.
My father is the thunder, my mother the dawn."

"I remember love and laughter upon the waters.
I played the flute beneath the bright moon.
I remember the heady smell of the ripe grain,
and the songs of the boatmen."

"I have always been made of stone."

"That was later. Now, of course,
Caesars come to gaze on me and wonder.
Their ladies write Greek poems on my feet.
But I remember life and the pain of life's ending."

"I remember nothing.
I am as I have always been."

Then the sun rises,
and the slowly heated stone
expands along some hidden fault,
and the stones begin to hum,
then sing, without words,
without any thought or remembrance at all.
Truly, this is the speech of the gods.

GLASTONBURY, 1995

Of course it was beautiful,
almost beyond words,
the Tor by moonlight,
the ruined tower at the summit
like a giant's index finger
thrust into the velvet sky.
Yes, I felt the magic then.
Earlier that day, in the town,
we had visited the Chalice Well,
and encountered an exotic survivor
of an ancient, lost world,
a genuine, psychedelically-clad,
barefoot hippie, doubtless an American,
here for the vibes.
We laughed at the crystals
for sale in the shop windows,
and such authentic, Arthurian paraphernalia
as a gaudy, gilt Buddha.
But on the Tor, at moonrise,
as we wound our way slowly up
the steep path where so many thousands
had trod before us,

on one of those rare, clear nights
when all of southern England
is spread out before you in the darkness
beneath the brilliant stars,
I saw things very differently.
A small group had gathered in the tower.
Someone played upon that most characteristic
of Celtic instruments, the diggery-do,
and the sound was low and soft and somber,
like a wind summoned and tamed by Merlin.
Someone else danced, a quiet shuffle.
I could well believe, then,
that here amid the Summer Country,
the Otherworld was very close,
and the hill beneath our feet
could, at any moment,
split open like a ripe fruit,
spewing forth dragons,
and the hosts of awakened heroes,
resplendent in their shining armor
by silver moonlight.
Yes, I felt it then.

THE COPYIST (ANNO DOMINI 700)

I thought that in this remote place,
hearing only the wind and the sea
and the cries of birds,
as my pen traced out slowly
the words of men long dead,
I would at last apprehend
the voiceless harmony of God.

But I find my cell a-babble with voices:
Strange gods, other gods, demons spoke,
rising up out of the very letters I traced,
their voices like beautiful thunder.
My soul trembled. I gazed, in my dreams,
into the heart of a dragon.
Dreaming while still awake,
I flew on wings amid the stars.

Great Caesar sat with me through the night
expounding on treachery, intrigue, and power,
and how even good men prove fickle in their hearts.
Proud Alexander, like the rising sun,

greeted the dawn in glory.
Orpheus played his lyre for me,
on his journey into the deathlands.
Even his pain was beautiful,
when the nymphs tore him limb from limb.
I have encountered monsters,
prodigies, and transformations,
a man become an ass,
an ass become a man,
a thing that is neither man nor bull,
and yet both, and bloody heroes,
who hurl their gleaming spears into the sun.

I was afraid.
I sought to silence them all,
by touching the page
to the candle's flame.
But the voices are in my head now.
Around me the flickering shadows pace,
thick with ghosts.
Now I am the shadow and I am the ghost.

Such is my confession.
This is my prayer:
that I should come to love
my damnation,
and follow strange gods,
into the unknowable dark,
and hear the song the sirens sing.

Last Supper (After Petronius)

Eat my corpse.
At the end of the *Satyricon*,
the dying rich man so commands
the sycophants and fortune-seekers
who swarm around him like flies.
If they wish to inherit his fortune,
then all they have to do
is endure a little unpleasantness,
which might even be mitigated
by a particularly tasty sauce.
(In the Fellini film we last see them
sitting around the funeral bier,
glumly chewing.)

But I think there's more to it than that.
They're terrified, all of them,
that what they've made
supper and sacrament of,
is the void itself, the awful nothingness
which fills their hearts and the whole universe,
the inescapable dread that none of them,

at their own funerals,
will even rate a sandwich.

CAUTIONARY TALE

Jack Sprat would eat no fat.
His wife would eat no lean.
Mrs. Sprat died in her late thirties
of a combination of diabetes,
high blood pressure, and heart failure.

Her husband outlived her by almost four decades.
He never remarried.

SONG OF A FORGOTTEN GOD

Out of the winter's mud and leaves,
out of the dark and the cold,
out of ancient memory, I am born,
an ancient and hobbled man,
with my naked limbs stretched upon the ground
as pale as the waning Moon,
yet I am newly come into the world,
and I rise dancing against the Sun.

Amid the forest in springtime,
amid the soothing, soft rains,
amid the fervid, growing green,
all clad in its living leaves,
with Moon-pale hair and beard grown dark,
I rage and run with the beasts,
the perilous father of all that I meet,
dancing, dancing against the Sun.

Now in the summer's beatific heat,
now along dusty roads,
now amid fields of ripening corn,
clothed in brown hides I come,

proud and strong, with Moon-bloody hands,
into the cities of men
stranger to all, yet friend to all,
and I am dancing against the Sun.

After the autumn's leaves have turned,
after the harvest is done,
after the flocks have come home from the hill,
beardless on a battlefield,
in the ravaging light of the Moon,
an innocent, beautiful, smooth-limbed child,
I lie down in death,
and still I'm dancing against the Sun.

We Have Cast Their Idols Down

We have cast their idols down,
trampled gods into the dust,
seized the loot of offerings,
made sport of slaughtered priests.
Now *our* gods stand in carven stone,
serene, eternal, gods to whom
we dedicate our swords.

Yet sunlight and shadow
that fall upon these,
are the same, are the same.
The rain, the leaves, the grit
between marble toes,
are the same, are the same.

We have cast their idols down,
trampled gods into the dust.

A Barbaric Song

Whet our swords for ravens' feasting!
Open wide the doors of Hell!
'Tis the dawn of ravens' feasting,
time of doom and omens fell!

Draw our swords for ravens' feasting!
Shields will split and skulls will crack!
Bring the noon of ravens' feasting!
Heroes strike, the skies turn black!

Sunset of the ravens' feasting!
Broken swords in bloody hands!
Heap the flesh for ravens' feasting!
Ghosts flee howling through the night!

WHEN WE THINK UPON THE KINGS OF OLD

When we think upon the kings of old,
the splendid warriors, lords of men,
with golden crowns and golden robes,
palaces grand and the loot of many lands
spread before their feet like apples
blown out of trees by a mighty wind,
their armies as irresistible as tide,
sent forth at a word or the wave of a hand,
it is not that we flatter ourselves to think,
that we might ever possess such things;
but we can imagine losing them,
for each of us, like Xerxes, Alexander, or Caesar,
hears the same footstep in the darkened hall,
the same clink of metal, or sighing night breeze,
when the assassin comes
to rob us of everything.

Justinian's Demon (Anno Domini 560)

The libel has been around for years,
that our lord Justinian,
ever victorious Augustus,
even as he reconquered the lands
that are rightfully Roman,
even as he gave the laws
and raised the splendid Hagia Sophia
to the glory of God,
entertained, on his left side,
a black and crouching thing,
man-shaped, but without any face at all,
a familiar spirit, which inspired
and directed all his actions
so that it might grow fat
on the blood of millions,
spilt in endless wars,
and work the ruin of all mankind.
Sometimes, they say, it took the shape
of the whore-empress, Theodora —
that's all she ever was, not human,
but the shadow of an infernal shadow —

and together the two of them
mocked the name of Christ.
A palace servant even claimed
to have seen the thing,
when he came into his master's bedroom
unexpectedly, bearing a lamp.

But such things are vulgar lies.
It was only long after his beloved was dead,
when he understood how alone he was,
when all his victories had become bitter dust,
when even his great church was filled with echoes,
and both the way to Heaven and the path of destiny
were clouded in his sight,
that the darkness at the emperor's left hand
began to speak, indeed, in Theodora's voice.

I THINK THAT WE ARE WITCHES NOW

We have our little secrets, you and I,
riding to meet the Black Man on the moor,
signing our names in his terrible book,
cavorting naked at the Sabbat.

I think that we are witches now.

But these are antics for the young,
who still have the energy
for all that cavorting,
not to mention spells, notions, and potions.

I think that we are witches now.

When I married late, a teenager into my forties,
I knew life would be full of surprises,
and little adjustments,
but I swear by Him Below,
that when you led me onto the roof at midnight,
both of us in our pajamas,
I was the one who protested, hey,
we're middle-aged and respectable, and

what will the neighbors think?
But you only laughed, and dropped off the edge,
backward, like a diver off a boat,
and I screamed, "No, don't!"
because I thought I'd lost you.
Then you laughed again, floating in the air,
your bathrobe flapping like a cloak.
You held out your hands,
and I took them,
and stepped into the air.

I think that we are witches now.

Lying in the cardiac ward brings a certain maturity,
even if the nurses call me "The kid."
It changes one's perspective.
A threshold has been crossed.
I could use some notions and potions right away.
But still I wait for you to tell me
that we shall soar through the night,
with or without brooms,
and dance till dawn on some black mountaintop.
Tell me we can still do it, please.

I think that we are witches now.

IS THERE SURVIVOR'S GUILT IN HEAVEN?

Is there survivor's guilt in Heaven?
Suppose you go searching
through all the wide, bright fields of Elysium,
and, in some immeasurable smidgen of Eternity,
manage to collar everyone who could possibly know,
"Where is so-and-so?" and the answer
is a sad shake of the head and the whisper,
"Not here"?
It might have been your nice Uncle Morris,
a delightful storyteller to the children,
generous, loving, good to his mother,
a loyal friend, funny, forgiving,
patient with kvetches;
"A saint! A living saint!" people used to say of him.
But Uncle Morris died of a heart attack
in the arms of a hooker,
with an ill-considered blasphemy on his lips,
and is now, quite literally, toast.
How are we supposed to feel
about friends who didn't make it,
colleagues, even a beloved spouse or child,
or a parent, with just one bad habit,

a little careless at the end,
now screaming in flames forever
while we, the lucky ones,
are supposed to sit back, strum our harps,
and enjoy ourselves?
Are we supposed to just forget about it?

Do they have support groups in Heaven,
to provide help and healing for the lady
mad with grief when her beloved
slipped away into the flames the way
Leonardo DiCaprio did into the dark waters
at the end of *Titanic*?
Is there some solemn, gentle-voiced therapist
who tells her it's part of the Plan,
and she shouldn't gaze searchingly down,
over the rim of Paradise
because that sort of thing
is a blemish on perfection?

Are there subversive cells in Heaven,
huddled bands of secretly sorrowing,
forlorn lovers, or grown-up kids,
who'd just like to hear another
of Uncle Morris's stories,
plotting and planning,
in the shadow of the Beatific Vision,
to lower a ladder down among the Damned,
and rescue, at least, a few?

Or is it just that as we enter
through the Pearly Gates,

we believe what we're told
and check compassion at the door?

Intelligent Design

Death is the engine of evolution.
That is its secret,
that, you, I, nations, species,
even God himself must perish
to make way for the new
and improved versions.
Selfish immortality
would be the greater death,
stagnation in the face
of eternal change.
Even God himself
must go.

LUCID DREAMING

The pages of the book over which I have fallen asleep
darken, and the room fills with smoke.
My first impulse is to sniff
and find out what's burning,
but I know perfectly well that I am dreaming,
and so am unconcerned.
The time of revelations is at hand.

Then I'm watching the conclusion of a movie,
a comedy, I think:
rural scene, colonial house with a wall,
seen from across a lake.
And a voice-over says portentously,
Gradually, all his paranoid notions came true,
even as the dragonflies and painted turtles in the lake
grow huge, morph into not-very-convincing,
rubbery dinosaurs,
which devour one another for a while,
then lumber up out of the lake,
crashing through the wall, into the house.
Screams. Falling debris.
The house topples as dinosaurs swarm through it.

Two lovers leap out one of the windows,
embrace tearfully on the ground,
and the house falls on them.
Now the dinosaurs plow through the house next door,
in an avalanche of stones and wood and screaming
people (including children),
a pyroclastic flow of disaster and death,
rushing right at the viewer,
seeming to burst out of the screen,
into the theater.
What a neat illusion.
A mesh of some sort holds it all back.
Wires spark and snap.
Two uniformed attendants
(also part of the picture, *another neat trick)*
reassure the audience,
"Don't worry, it's all part of the story,"
and they grab hold of the wire-mesh
and swing the entire image around to the side,
then haul it away on a flatbed truck.
This replaced by:
rural scene, a dusty road straight ahead,
another, perpendicular to the first,
vanishes behind hedges, right.
It's the end of the movie.
The hero whistles for his dog,
a very dim-witted dachshund.
Several other dogs appear first,
disappearing behind the hedge.
At last the dachshund waddles after them,
followed by a stop-motion stegosaurus.
We continue to gaze down that dusty road.

In the distance, several cars and a truck crash,
piling up like the dinos in the lake,
as the voice of one of the attendants remarks,
*"If you are wondering what this means,
so are we."*
This then is the revelation.
All the clues have been provided.
It is the answer.
But what is the question?
Not whether I have awakened,
but whether I ever went to sleep.

A FURTHER VOYAGE TO BYZANTIUM

So you come at last
to the holy city of Byzantium.
There are no golden birds singing in metal trees,
only muffled hoofbeats, shouts, and the occasional thwack
of boys playing a game like polo
in the grassy ruin of the Hippodrome,
their cries like crows, faint and far away,
at the end of a long summer's day.
You pass street after street of silent, roofless houses,
and cross fields where the pavement has been torn up
to plant crops, as if no city of Byzantium existed at all.
This is a place of ghosts, of memories,
of the echoes of great names no longer spoken aloud.
In Hagia Sophia, yes, you can still feel the shiver
of miracles from another age, and gaze up in amazement
at the glowing mosaics of saints and emperors,
caught in the last gleam of sunset,
strangers, like yourself, from out of the deeps of time.
Step back to see better. Plaster crunches underfoot.

Meanwhile, in Blachernai Palace,
the last, loyal guardian of the Ancient Word,

which descends upon holy Byzantium directly from Christ,
and somewhat more obscurely from Julius Caesar,
waits patiently for the end.
This is a city for old men,
at the precise moment when the dream
passes out of the body and becomes
truly and forever a dream.

PART TWO

THE MATTER OF BRITAIN

Sir Canis de Nobody

The thunder and the glory of it!
The hot spring day, the brilliant sky,
the tourney ground at Camelot:
a prideful fool athirst for fame,
I entered in the lists,
in armor stolen shamefully
from dead men left in fields.
I would not raise my visor
nor give out any name,
for No One's face is best not seen
nor the name of Nothing heard.

The thunder and the glory of it!
All eyes were turned, the fairground still,
the King looked quite amazed,
but then his noble, gracious queen,
whispered in his ear,
"A knight unknown, on quest, no doubt,
bound by exotic vows!"
"Ah, yes, I see," the king replied,
"there's quite a lot of that.
Quests and vows are all the rage,

so let the games begin!"

The thunder and the glory of it!
The trumpets blared, the pennons streamed,
my bold steed bravely charged
straight up against Sir Lancelot —
I landed on my butt!
"So kick me now!" I cried aloud,
"for I am Fortune's dog!"
"Yes, that you are!" sly Merlin said,
and magicked me away,
so when they claimed my iron hide,
I'm nowhere to be found.

The thunder and the glory of it!
A steely-haired, long-legged hound,
I had found my place.
I sat with pride by his right foot
beneath King Arthur's table.
or raced with him upon the hunt
to catch the fleeing hart.
I say he loved me; late at night,
he'd scratch behind my ears
and whisper softly, secret things
of statecraft and of crowns.

Thunder and glory! Glory and Thunder!
On came the charging hosts,
to victory at Badon Hill,
against the heathen foe,
I fought at Arthur's side that day
and tasted Saxon blood!

I saw my share of miracles,
and rogue knights brought to heel,
ladies saved, giants slain,
all in the thundering and strife
that men call Chivalry.

Glory there was, the thunder of dread,
upon that Pentecost:
The Grail appeared within the hall
and each man found his plate
heaped on high with tasty meats
(I gnawed a splendid bone!)
But our lord Arthur wept full sore,
for these were sinful men
who swore this quest, and most would die,
and never more be gathered here
to dine again as friends.

Thunder yes, but glory none,
at least as I could see,
when Arthur's queen betrayed him
and was condemned to burn.
I yelped and ran between men's legs
when charged Sir Lancelot:
old comrades, fellows, friends he slew;
the rest cried out for blood,
urged on by traitor Mordred,
who gained no crown, but only death
on Camlann's sodden ground.

I found the king, then, dying,
he scratched behind my ears,

and whispered out his many sins.
Oh God, could I but speak!
"Sir Hound," he said, "you are the last,
most faithful of them all . . ."
Did he know? His hand went limp;
and four queens bore him off.
Then howling by a misty shore
I chased my wretched tail,
perhaps for want of glory.

When I became a man again,
by gradual degree,
I crouched on hearths, lapped from a bowl,
was kicked about a lot.
Yet eloquent, I'll rise and speak,
recall the fading names
of kings and wizards, maids and lords,
for I was *one* of them.
"Sir Hound" I'm dubbed, as much a knight
as sainted Galahad!
And in my words there's thunder still,
and glory, yes there's glory!

THE FINAL MYSTERY OF KING ARTHUR

They took him back.
After the thunder of Camlann,
after he'd spitted Mordred on a spear
and suffered his own grievous wound,
the three queens from the otherworld
snatched him away like a chess piece off the board,
like a borrowing, now returned.
We see them standing over him in the barge,
their hands upraised in despair or supplication,
like Virgin Marys in holy icons.
So Arthur vanished toward Avalon,
out of all human understanding,
leaving behind only the irresolvable enigma
of his true origin, nature, and substance.
Was he even truly a man,
or a miracle made into shadowy flesh
like some phantom, Monophysite Christ,
whom no nail ever pierced,
an illusion upon the cross?
Was Arthur like that,
a Word come among us for a time,
as insubstantial as smoke or dew?

Even the men who broke bread with him
or tilted with him upon the field,
or felt the bite of his sword,
might wonder, not at his disappearance and death,
but whether he was ever alive at all.

AMID THE FIELD OF CORPSES

Amid the field of corpses,
at Camlann, after both armies
had so improbably suffered
one hundred percent casualties,
as he stood exhausted and alone,
but for Sir Bedivere, who was wounded,
and Sir Lucan the Butler, who was worse,
did Arthur pause to wonder whether
it had all been worth it?
When he came face-to-face
with the blood-stained apparition
of that sin of his flesh, his own son,
was it possible to forgive?
By best report, what he actually did
was shout, "Traitor, thy death-day has come!"
and spit Mordred on a spear
even as he received his own death-wound.
Then, from the strain of helping him up off the ground,
Lucan's guts fell out, and Lucan died at the feet
of his brother, Bedivere, while Bedivere and Arthur wept.

The King's thoughts after that were like bright colors

running together: Worth it? Forgive?
God, how his head hurt...maybe Christ himself,
could forgive, but not a man who has just seen all
his friends die...Guinevere! The miracle of the Grail!
...all those wrongs righted, if only for
a little while...how can there be
light without shadow, joy without sorrow...?

Then Bedivere whispered to him:
"Just think, My Lord, of the *story*,
which will be on men's tongues *forever*."
And Bedivere knew that was a sin,
because Arthur, on the threshold of salvation,
should have been thinking about God, not
distracted by vanity and little white lies
told to ease the immediate pain.
But God surely forgave Bedivere,
because the lies were an act of mercy,
and they weren't even lies, after all.

SIR BOSS REMEMBERED

(BY THE SURVIVORS OF *A CONNECTICUT YANKEE IN KING ARTHUR'S COURT*)

CLARENCE:

We few, we proud and select few,
we vanishing few,
burdened by his confidences,
his industry, his gimcracks —
To think that we served him with such zeal!

THE COMMONS OF ENGLAND:

The Fiend! The Fiend! The very Devil incarnate!

CLARENCE:

He slaughtered countless thousands out of spite,
in what he described as a short and boring interval.
I think that he had become as unfeeling
as the steel armor he would not deign to wear.

THE COMMONS:

The serpent sent among us!

SANDY:

No, I think he could still love.
I think loved me for a time,
and that love nearly redeemed him.

CLARENCE:

Nearly is not good enough.
If he taught me anything, it was precision,
that exasperated mechanic who smashed all he'd built
because it did not please him,
and didn't give a God-damn about the rest of us,
that monstrous drillmaster who said, "These dolts will
never march lockstep, as proper cogs in *my* machine, so
to Hell with them all."
And to Hell he sent us.

SANDY:

I saw tenderness in his eyes
when our child was ill.

CLARENCE:

Or was it mere possessiveness,
the fear that something that was *his*
might be taken from him?

SANDY:

I wept for him.

CLARENCE:

So too did Attila the Hun's wife weep for him,
most extravagantly, as is written in a book —

SANDY:

That is nothing to me.

CLARENCE:

Because he didn't teach you to read, did he,
any more than he taught his horse or his dog,
or anything else he already owned?

SANDY:

I saw goodness in him.

CLARENCE:

I'll tell you what *I* saw.
I saw Satan trying to be God,
like a child too small to fill his father's shoes,
and so he picks up one of those shoes,
and smashes everything in sight.
I saw it all in one, terrifying instant,
at the tourney, when things got serious at last,

and with six-guns blazing he neatly potted
near a dozen knights.
I saw it in his eyes,
no regret that he'd had to do such a thing,
nor anger, nor even the legitimate triumph of victory,
but the malicious, unholy glee
of the small child who *has* smashed what there is to smash,
and now hefts his father's shoe in his hands
like a favorite toy.
He was truly happy then,
in that instant, as he sinned the sin of Cain.

SANDY:

Nevertheless, I mourned for him.

CLARENCE:

Death take me! I can't get it out of my mind!
In the end I became a monk,
for the healing of my soul,
orphaned like all the rest,
with nothing to do but bury the countless dead,
unable to find any comfort for the living,
and certain of my own damnation,
because I had found playing his game
and building his horrible engines
so much fun.

COMMONS:

The Fiend! God save us from the return of such a one!

PART THREE

POST-HOMERICA

THEY SURE EAT A LOT IN EPICS

They sure eat a lot in epics.
The Greek heroes seem to spend
more than half their time feasting,
all their comings and goings
celebrated for thousands of lines
about pigs or oxen slaughtered,
the hind-quarters sacrificed to Zeus,
the rest gorged upon amid
whole oceans of alcoholic beverage —
a wine-dark sea indeed! —
with more than a few drops spilled out
in libation to the gods.

Homer's world must have been noted
for sticky floors, but not, I think,
for rising blood-pressure, diabetes,
or cirrhosis of the liver,
or even, with a few memorable exceptions,
gray beards.

There was no old age for Agamemnon,
murdered on his own doorstep

as he came home from the war.
Achilles, the James Dean of his day,
made the choice
to live fast and die young.
Odysseus's entire crew,
when they butchered the cattle of the Sun
and earned themselves a thunderbolt,
quite literally gave their lives
for one last outdoor barbecue.

More certainly than any philosophers,
those men knew how fleeting
are the things of this world,
how soon the taste of the wine
will fade into nothingness,
and the beef become as dust.
Therefore the epic hero
embraces the whole world
and shoves it into his mouth
as fast as possible
without concern for spreading waistlines
or the condition of his arteries.
His mouth and belly will be empty again,
soon enough, in the dark,
in the cold, among the shades.

AFTER HOURS IN THE HALL OF HEROES

I.

The epic is done,
the great feast,
the sacrifices in thanksgiving,
the athletic contests,
and maybe a ritual duel or two,
all concluded, the clangor of arms
faded beyond echo,
smoke stagnant beneath the roofbeams,
spears, shields, and plume-crested helmets
neatly hung in rows along the walls,
gleaming in the dying firelight,
while here and there
among the tables and benches,
one or two men still nurse their cups,
or play silent, obscure games,
with bones and dice, fatalistically
divining their own futures, perhaps,
or else just bored.
The room echoes with snores,
and all you see, in the gloom,

are a bunch of beefy guys,
their bodies gleaming with sweat and spilled wine,
a few with gray-streaked beards and
getting a little soft around the waist,
all of them heaped about higgledy-piggledy
like so many sacks of unwashed laundry.

II.

This is the hour when the inner, doubting voice
whispers, *Lies, all lies*,
malevolently suggesting that these are *not* the darlings of destiny,
just a bunch of thugs — pirates, rapists, and murderers —
their mighty deeds consisting mostly of the slaughter
of poor villagers and the theft of a few scrawny cattle,
these crimes magnified into something glorious
by villainous bards who would have us believe
that upon such squalid butcheries
the fate of the universe somehow depends,
and that the very gods,
leaning forward on their cloudy thrones,
deign to follow the story intently,
its more exciting episodes being, of course,
but reflections of greater, heavenly conflict,
as if these gods actually exist,
and put the heroes through their arbitrary paces
like bones and dice rolled on a tabletop,
in some inscrutable game.
But if the reality is merely
stolen cattle, corpses left behind,
and weeping children, dragged off into slavery,

then no intelligence directs this sorry spectacle,
and there's only dust in the end,
and the remorseless dark.

III.

It is in hearing this
(as all of them do,
even in their stupor),
as each warrior dreads
in the secret caverns of his heart,
that the words might be true,
that the real test of courage comes.
With no certainty of rewards in Elysium,
these men keep the beautiful myths alive,
defending us all against
the whispering voice and devouring dark.
Only then are they true heroes,
deserving of fame and worthy of praise.

HELEN RETURNS TO TROY

The Greeks did not know
this part of the story:
that Helen in her old age,
reports of her demise still
somewhat exaggerated,
visited the ruins of Troy,
and wept.
Her beauty was gone by then,
poured out and wasted,
like wine from a discarded vessel;
yet still she possessed
an undeniable, indefinable grandeur
like the ancient, weathered statue
of a goddess, seen at twilight.
Indeed, a child of the barbarians
asked her if she were a goddess,
and she replied sadly, no,
though she had known much
of gods and goddesses in her day.
The child knew all about them too:
Aren't they with us every day,
in the sun and the wind and the rain?

But when Helen looked, she saw only
the setting sun, the gathering dark,
the dust stirred up, lightning flickering
on the horizon from the arrival
of a sudden, summer storm.
Nothing more than that.
And so she wept, out of relief
that the Olympians
might finally leave her alone,
that they no longer cared,
that she was only Helen now,
and not "of Troy."

I DREAMED THAT I SAILED IN A SHIP OF HEROES

I dreamed that I sailed in a ship of heroes,
across a wine-dark sea as smooth as polished glass.
The wind bellied the sail,
but there was no strength in it.
So we rowed in silence,
against the piercing cold,
until we came to the shores of Death,
and there debarked on the bone-pale sand,
our bright armor gleaming,
shields clattering, swords drawn,
the horsehair crests of our helmets rippling
in that same impotent breeze.
We fought our way inland,
overwhelming Hades's legions, cutting them down like
wheat,
their thick, stagnant blood offered in libation
to the Dark God and the Veiled Queen,
whose thrones proved empty when at last
we broke into the black palace at the center of Hell.
Then all of us milled about

in confusion at the moment of victory,
until each man heard a familiar voice,
or felt a gentle, remembered touch,
which led him away into the darkness.

I found my father there in the Underworld.
He sat in the same hospital bed where I'd seen him,
on the last day when he was alive,
in a sunny hospital room in Florida.
He was in good cheer, and full of stories,
but in a reflective moment he reminded me
that elders, particularly parents,
are our last line of defense,
and when they're gone,
it is each of us who stands unprotected
in the front line of a battle no one can win.
"Dad, did you fall in the struggle?" I asked.
He replied, "No, I struggled in the fall."
And as I struggled to figure that one out,
I awoke, to the sound of the alarm-clock ticking,
and the wind fluttering calendar pages.

The Gods Rage at Us

The gods rage at us,
burning with jealousy
precisely because we are mortal,
because, on the threshold of death,
we live our lives more intensely,
our senses are more keen,
our thoughts more profound,
our every twitch and sneeze
rich in complexities they
cannot begin to comprehend.
We are their tea-leaves, their auguries;
they attempt to discover some meaning
to *their* pointless existence
by the examination of *our* entrails;
but it doesn't work.
Therefore heroes perish messily,
cities burn, plagues sweep away first-born sons,
whole nations cry out in anguish,
as the deaf gods strain for something
they'll never, ever hear.

THE COMPANION'S TALE

On the bank of the black river
we made our camp,
and the hero sat in the firelight,
his breastplate and helmet gleaming,
the helmet worn down over his face,
his eyes alone visible, gleaming.
For my instruction, he recounted
the stages of our journey thus far:
the haunted forest, the perilous crags,
the number of enemies we had slain.
It was only after we had
overpowered the ferryman,
stolen his boat,
and reached the opposite shore,
that my master admitted
that only one of us could return,
it being the nature of our mission,
and entirely too bad,
that blood must be spilled
to appease the spirits of this land
if ever we were to attain
the secret of the place,

for the benefit of mankind.

I swear to you it was because
I loved my master perfectly,
and desired above all things,
that the glory of his life
remain untarnished by treachery,
that I ran him through with my sword,
and proceeded past the murmuring ghosts
that lapped up his blood like dogs,
and broke down the doors of the infernal palace
and confront the Lord of Death on his dark throne.
There he sat, his helmet covering his face,
helmet and breastplate agleam by firelight,
and he yielded up to me his secret:
that I should return into the world,
and commit countless acts
of violence and horror
in the guise of virtue,
until I should inspire some apprentice
to love me so much
that he would give me release.

NEAR THE END OF THE EPIC

Near the end of the epic,
on the eve of the last battle,
the heroes gather for a final feast,
where there will be drinking and boasting
on, indeed, an epic scale,
while the regular guys,
not the ones whose names
will be made eternal with glory,
but the also-rans, who wield
the forest of spears,
whose clamor of swords upon shields
speaks like thunder in the dawn,
these men will eat and swill
and make laconic remarks like,
"now that we have feasted,
so shall the ravens tomorrow,"
and then they'll sit around,
tossing knucklebones, or sharpening
their weapons, speaking fondly
to gleaming blades, which have names,
lying down for the last time
to a sleep from which they hope to awaken,

and if they dream of home, of loved ones,
of some trivial but fondly-recalled scene
from childhood, it does not matter,
because the villainous bards,
who turned this enterprise into an epic,
left that part out, not deigning to mention
the thousands of lives washed away like ashes
scattered on the seashore at the turning of the tide.
These are the truly great ones, worthy of fame
precisely because they don't have it,
hearts all the stronger, courage the greater,
as their numbers diminish.

ITHACA, AT LAST

The final mystery remains,
like a wound that will not heal:
Filled with sorrow for the deaths
of his entire crew,
without treasure or trophies
to show for his many years of wandering,
Odysseus, now supposedly grown wise,
having attained his beloved Ithaca at last,
immediately drowns the place in blood.
For the crime of staying overlong at his table,
and making eyes at his wife,
he slaughters the suitors
like a male lion cleaning out the pride
of his rival's progeny.
The resultant blood-feud
would have set off
a whole new epic of senseless carnage
had not the thunderbolt of Zeus
proclaimed that enough was finally enough.

So, did Odysseus learn anything at all
from his journeys, even in the Underworld,

when the ghosts of his dead sailors bewailed
how much better it is to be a slave's slave on Earth
than king over all the dead?

Not even Homer has a clue,
but perhaps Homer did not know,
that while Odysseus was in the Underworld,
a shadow detached itself from the greater darkness,
and whispered into the hero's ear,
"Nobody gets out of here unscathed,
not even you. Our Lord has never
forgiven Orpheus, who, you recall,
did not exactly live
happily ever after.
Do not flatter yourself to think
that you can do any better."

While he was in the Underworld,
Odysseus struck a deal,
maybe because he loved Penelope so much,
or because he was arrogant enough to think
he could wheedle out of it later,
or just because he was afraid,
the agreement being that only as long
as he satisfied Lord Hades
through other means,
would he himself be spared.

And the shadow accompanied him out of the Underworld.
It walked beside him upon the Earth.
It rejoiced in the blood of the suitors.
When Penelope saw it in his eyes,

she wept, knowing that she had lost him again.
She was not surprised when,
a few years later, restless Odysseus
gathered another crew and set sail
for the world's end, where the crafty shadow
made short work of them all.

By then, she was done with weeping.

PART FOUR

YESTERDAY'S TOMORROW

REMEMBERING THE FUTURE

We remember the future,
the bright, curving horizons gleaming
on viewscreens against a backdrop of stars,
space-armored legions clanking
past rows of hulking machines
like enormous vacuum tubes
to confront the all-metal worlds:
planets armed and powered
as only planets can be,
and dropped out of hyperspace
like so many ping-pong balls.
We know that mankind will triumph
in the end, even as we know
that Mars with its blown-glass cities
and Venus with swamps and dinosaurs
are out there, waiting.
We are, after all, the race
that will rule the Sevagram,
whatever that is.

But time passes.
The future fades.

We look back on it fondly,
yet with little conviction.
How very selfish to think
it was ever ours alone.
No, once you and I
have long since been absorbed
into the Cosmic Overmind,
or are just specks of dust
in a Lensman's wake,
the future will remain.
Let us remember it fondly, then,
in great detail,
and pass it on,
like the treasure that it is,
to our children.

AS WE JOURNEYED TOWARD THE CENTER OF THE GALACTIC EMPIRE

1.

As we journeyed toward the center
of the Galactic Empire,
we encountered, first, the Barrier Worlds,
scattered along the rim,
armor-plated, bristling with weapons,
their force-shields flickering
like mad auroras.
But we were allowed to pass,
because the voice of the Emperor was within us,
serene and constant through the ether,
the voice of order, assurance, and of eternity,
which in primitive times, might have been called
the voice of God, saying, "Let them come to us,
to bear witness to our glory."

2.

As we journeyed toward the center
of the Galactic Empire,

we passed farming worlds, green and blue and white,
around ten thousand suns, and great planet-cities;
and a million golden spaceships swarmed like sparrows,
the babble of their commerce a hymn of praise.
Closer in, whole systems had been shaped
into the likenesses of emperors who once were;
immense effigies floating in the dark,
half-lit by the stars they circled.

3.

As we journeyed toward the center
of the Galactic Empire,
after a while the people were no longer human,
evolved far beyond mere humanity,
winged beings, levitating brains, bio-machines,
and sentient spheres of light,
their cities fallen into decay
after their ancient ancestors
had set forth to found the Galactic Empire.

4.

As we reached the center
of the Galactic Empire,
fifty thousand light-years in,
the voice of the Emperor faded into silence,
and we could only appreciate the irony,
that the Galactic Empire is itself,
a ripple spreading out
from a core ultimately wiped clean of life
by fire and radiation and the tides of time.

There was nothing to do then but pause,
and wait a billion years,
for the evolution of thinking creatures
to begin again.

AT THE CONCLUSION OF AN INTERSTELLAR WAR

Of course we won.
Earth's clever scientists
deftly disassembled your fiendish devices,
built shields against your rays,
rays against your clanking machines,
then knocked your moon-sized dreadnoughts
out of the sky, blowing them
to smithereens and crackling sparks.
In the end, our grim-jawed,
space-armored heroes trampled
the dust of your home world
into, well, more dust,
shouting as they did, "Die, alien scum!
Free Men" — a term which includes women —
"are coming to kill you!"

It's a shame
that we couldn't have shared
what eons of alternate evolution
crammed into your bulging brains
before we reduced them to jelly.

The perspectives would have been staggering,
to say nothing of the beauty of your ancient art,
the scroll books illuminated
when our ancestors were still in trees
now delicate as ash, and indecipherable.
Your million lost Shakespeares
could have been saved
if only you hadn't tried
to abduct our women
(a term which includes only women),
steal our water and air,
plow our cities under to plant your garden,
and turn us into zombie-slaves
with mind-controlling slugs on our backs.
It *was* your fault, you know.

So now we can only
write "KILROY WAS HERE"
on your enigmatic ruins,
put up our billboards and hotdog stands,
express romantic longings and crackpot theories,
compose sad little poems,
and forget.

THE LAST MESSAGE IN A BOTTLE FROM THE LOST VALLEY OF FONGO-FONGO

It's all true:

There's a McDonald's in Kôr these days.
Ayesha's moved to California,
where she earns big bucks channeling
reincarnated lovers while waiting
for the A.M.A. to approve
her line of Immortal Flame Health Boutiques.

La of Opar's gone Feminist.
She was on *Oprah* the other night,
plugging her new book,
I Was the Ape-Man's Lust Object.
Jane plans to sue for divorce.

"Shangri-La has been completely liberated,"
the Chinese *People's Daily* reports.

And *Variety* says that Spielberg plans
to shoot *Jurassic Park* at the Challenger Ranch
in Mato Grasso.

Enough is enough!
Our (politically incorrect) White Goddess Queen decrees
that her realm shall remain lost forever,
retreating like a tide
into legend and memory, into myth.
Better to be a dream
than a Third World backwater.

Sacrifices to the volcano god continue as always,
and pith-helmeted strangers are killed on sight.

AT THE EARTH'S CORE

Dante was right,
Burroughs was wrong,
and so when
David Innes and Abner Perry
reached their destination
the iron mole broke through,
not into a jungle landscape
with a strangely curved horizon
beneath a fiery, central sun,
but into a black, frozen lake,
where colossal Satan stood,
sunk to the waist and held fast,
grinding traitors in his massive jaws,
the only fire being the madness in his eyes.

What terrifying adventures they had,
trying to escape up through the Circles,
trying to explain to the demons
that there must be some mistake,
pitchforked back into the abyss
of soul and conscience,
until at last they understood

that the way out was *down*,
across the Devil's foul backside,
and, as gravity shifted, *up*,
along his hairy legs,
into the unknown.
How they yearned to confront
mere dinosaurs then.

ALTERNATE HISTORIES

Even as Napoleon, Hitler, and Philip the Second
marched triumphantly into London,
as Caesar escaped assassination
and conquered the whole East,
and Grant died of tetanus
after stepping on a nail at Vicksburg,
while time-travelers gave Frederick Barbarossa
an AK-47 and a life-jacket,
the stranger who might have been my friend,
whose colored coat I could not see clearly
in the mud and darkness,
lay beside me in a little hollow of ground,
coughing up blood, babbling of green fields,
and calling out some woman's name.
The light on the horizon
might have been a burning city,
or the sunrise, which for him,
at least, never came.

SCIENTIFIC ROMANCE

When we were master and mistress of the world,
when our airships soared like apocalyptic visions
above the helpless navies,
we could have erased whole cities,
even continents, at the touch of a lever,
with our bombs, gas, and radium rays,
forcing mankind to yield to our demands.
But, lacking any messianic agenda,
or the desire to slaughter anonymous strangers,
we merely voyaged on, admiring
the Alps and Himalayas gleaming like icy teeth,
and the brilliant moonlight on the clouds below.
I steered the great vessel; you held my hand steady,
while kings and kaisers trembled
at the thunder of our engines.
In the end, we dismissed all our minions
on good pensions, detonated the secret island base,
and in our old age, sat side by side
on cold winter's nights,
feeding plans and blueprints into the fire,
reminiscing about the times we had,
very much aware of what might happen

if such knowledge ever fell
into irresponsible hands.

NOTES

There are fewer notes this time than in *Groping Toward the Light* because a volume of my specifically historical poetry is planned by another publisher, and so I have gone lightly on the historical stuff, except where it gets explicitly eerie. But here are some observations that may be of interest:

Cemetery Tour, Montreal, Early November 2001.

This tour was given the evening after the World Fantasy convention that year. We went to Montreal's most ancient cemetery, at dusk, on a rainy evening. It was as atmospheric as any fantasy or horror writer could have wanted, and yet, particularly when we went into the newer, underground vaults that were as clean and polished as shopping malls, with the photographs of loved ones on the walls and, the candles flickering, I could not help but feel that we were intruding into something private, making light of someone else's still very active grief. Centuries' old spirits are used to this sort of thing, I am sure, but the recently dead are not.

The Spirit That Fled from Julian's Tent.

The Roman emperor Flavius Claudius Julianus, known to history as Julian the Apostate, is, next to Cicero and Julius Caesar, the most documented person of antiquity. Three volumes of the emperor's writings are available in the Loeb Classical Library, as are writings by his contemporaries Libanius and Ammianus Marcellinus. He was a nephew of Constantine the Great, but famously rejected Christianity and attempted to restore the old gods by creating a pagan church of his own invention, in which Neo-Platonism was fused with the kind of organization and aggressive good works that made Christianity so successful. He attempted to actually realize the ideal of the philosopher king in the person of himself, and to emulate the military prowess of Alexander the Great by invading Persia. This is where he ran into trouble, because, despite some notable victories early in his career, he was not as good a general as he thought he was. He was killed in a skirmish during the campaign, by a spear in the side, as he rushed to encourage his men during a sudden attack and forgot to put on his breastplate. The rumor did indeed spread that a spirit, representing the Genius of his regime, was seen to depart his tent shortly before he died. Ironically, this is a Persian concept. Julian has been a romantic hero for centuries, and the subject of many plays and novels, most notably those of Henrik Ibsen and Gore Vidal, respectively.

Edgar Allan Poe Nears His End.

Most of these details are lifted from Kenneth Silverman's

Edgar A Poe, Mournful and Never-ending Remembrance (1991), and of course from the enigmatic conclusion of "The Narrative of Arthur Gordon Pym." Poe, in the end, remains a mystery. Theories about his death are just theories. There will be more of them.

The Colossi of Memnon Near Thebes.

Actually they are statues of Amenhotep III, but the later ancients preferred to believe them to be images of the Greek hero Memnon, son of Aurora, the goddess of dawn. The statues had been damaged in an earthquake, so that at dawn, as the stones heated up, they vibrated and gave off a sound like the twanging of a harp. The "singing" statues were a popular tourist attraction in Roman times until the emperor Septimius Severus (193-211) ordered them repaired, whereupon they became forever silent. Like the ancients, I have not scrupled to let a few facts get in the way of a good story.

A Barbaric Song.

Discovered on an ancient tablet of *Hyboria's Greatest Hits* circa 10,000 B.C., this could be a pop tune from the era of Conan the Barbarian. Then again, maybe not.

Justinian's Demon.

All the racy, fantastic, or sinister stories about Justinian and Theodora come from one of the most fascinating of all ancient hatchet-jobs, the *Anecdota* or *Secret History* of Procopius. Procopius was perhaps trained as a physician and was a historian of genius, who wrote the official histories of the wars of Justinian, and also a book devoted to the emperor's buildings; but at least late in life he came to hate his master and view him as a fiend in human form, whose every action was motivated by a desire to ruin the Roman (Byzantine) Empire and increase the suffering of mankind. Possibly the immense cost in treasure and lives of Justinian's wars of reconquest, plus the catastrophic outbreak of bubonic plague in A.D. 542 (which must have been seen as a divine visitation), led Procopius to this view. Or else he was just a resentful man who could secretly nurse a grudge. The *Anecdota* of course could not be published in his (or Justinian's) lifetime.

I Think That We Are Witches Now.

I am surprised to realize, assembling this collection, that my poetry is far more directly autobiographical than my fiction. No, it wasn't a heart attack. It was hyperthyroidism. I actually collapsed at the airport on my way to a convention where I was to be, ironically, poet guest of honor. Whether or not I have levitated in my pajamas or signed the Black Man's book I refuse to divulge.

A Further Voyage to Byzantium.

An attempt to capture the moment when the 1,500-year-old dream of the Roman Empire lost its last, tenuous hold on reality and became entirely a myth, albeit a lively one for many centuries yet. The detail of the boys playing polo in the ruins of the Hippodrome comes from the account of a traveler to Constantinople in the mid-fifteenth century, just before the fall of the city to the Turks. The poem is an answer of sorts to Yeats, who describes (in "Sailing to Byzantium") a holy city which has put off the body altogether and become a realm of the spirit.

The Final Mystery of King Arthur.

The Monophysites (together with Docetists and Gnostics) held that Christ had only a divine nature, and that his humanity was an illusion. He didn't really suffer on the cross, but only seemed to. Arthur, as myth, seems no more substantial than that.

They Sure Eat a Lot in Epics.

The catastrophic beef barbecue is a key episode in *The Odyssey.* I owe to Theresa Nielsen-Hayden the observation that epics were designed to be recited at kingly feasts, and therefore had to give good food-value.

I Dreamed That I Sailed in a Ship of Heroes.

Autobiography again. When I last saw my father alive, he was indeed in a hospital in Florida, where he had survived bypass surgery with flying colors and was cheerfully discussing with the doctor where he was going to park his car in two weeks when he drove in for a checkup. So I flew home in good spirits. He died the next day of a sudden blood clot to the heart.

Ithaca, At Last.

I have always suspected that the violence of Odysseus toward the suitors appealed to something primal and primitive in the ancient Greeks which we can never comprehend. We are not they. Odysseus did not merely say, "Okay, I'm home. Party's over. Everybody out and don't take the silverware." No, he had to kill *all of them* to reassert himself. The tale that Odysseus became restless again and perished on a voyage to the world's end is told in Dante's *Purgatorio.*

Remembering the Future.

My most successful poem, at least financially, as it won me a $100 prize and a free breakfast when the readers of *Isaac Asimov's SF* voted it best of the year for 2006. The bit about armed planets is from Doc Smith's *Second Stage Lensmen*, by way of a paragraph quoted in Fritz Leiber's *The Wanderer.* Otherwise I tried to make the imagery here sound like a series of Hubert Rogers covers from *Astounding* of the Golden Age. That future is in the past now, but it is still the core myth of science fiction.

At the Conclusion of an Interstellar War.

Possibly some readers need to be told that "Kilroy was here" was a ubiquitous graffito that followed the American troops through Europe during World War II. Nobody knows who Kilroy was or how it started, though there are explanations.

The Last Message in a Bottle from the Lost Valley of Fongo-Fongo.

See, especially, *She* by H. Rider Haggard, *Tarzan and the Jewels of Opar* by Edgar Rice Burroughs, and *Lost Horizon* by James Hilton. Lost cities and races have indeed vanished away in the modern world, because there are no explored parts of the Earth left in which to discover them.

At the Earth's Core.

David Innes and Abner Perry are the heroes of Edgar Rice Burroughs's *At the Earth's Core*, *Pellucidar*, etc. But Dante placed Satan's frozen lake at the center of the earth. They both can't be right.

ACKNOWLEDGMENTS

These poems have previously published as follows:

Denying Ghosts first appeared in *Star*Line*, March/April 2004. Copyright © 2004 by Darrell Schweitzer.

Cemetery Tour, Montreal, Early November 2001 first appeared in *Weird Tales* #336, Fall 2004. Copyright © 2004 by Terminus Publishing Co., Inc.

Death Is the Great Unwinding first appeared in *The Book of Dark Wisdom* #7, Fall 2005. Copyright © 2005 by Elder Signs Press.

We Dead Outnumber the Living, You Know first appeared in *Flesh and Blood* #11. Copyright © 2003 by Darrell Schweitzer.

I Miss the Night Sky is published here for the first time. Copyright © 2008 by Darrell Schweitzer.

Look How the Moonlight Has Made Us Young Again first appeared in *Dreams of Decadence* #14, Summer 2001. Copyright © 2001 by DNA Publications.

Those That Do Not Find Their Way into Elfland first appeared in *Talebones* #25. Copyright © 2002 by Talebones Magazine.

Cautionary Tale appears here for the first time. Copyright © 2008 by Darrell Schweitzer.

Song of a Forgotten God first appeared in *Talebones #21*, Spring 2001. Copyright © 2001 by Talebones Magazine.

We Have Cast Their Idols Down first appeared in *The Cimmerian*, October 2006. Copyright © 2006 by Darrell Schweitzer

A Barbaric Song first appeared in *The Cimmerian*, June 2006. Copyright © 2006 by Darrell Schweitzer

When We Think Upon the Kings of Old first appeared in *The Cimmerian*, February 2006. Copyright © 2006 by Darrell Schweitzer.

Justinian's Demon appeared in a somewhat different form in *Weird Tales* #339, March/April 2006. Copyright © 2006 by Wildside Press.

I Think That We Are Witches Now first appeared in *Star*Line*, November/Dec 2000. Copyright © 2000 by Darrell Schweitzer

Is There Survivor's Guilt in Heaven? first appeared in *Dreams and Nightmares* #62. Copyright © 2002 by Darrell Schweitzer.

Intelligent Design appears here for the first time. Copyright © 2008 by Darrell Schweitzer.

Lucid Dreaming first appeared in *Mythic Delirium* #5. Copyright © 2001 by Darrell Schweitzer.

A Further Voyage to Byzantium first appeared in *Star*Line*, May/June 2003. Copyright © 2003 by Darrell Schweitzer.

Sir Canis de Nobody first appeared in *Star*Line*, November/December 2002. Copyright © 2002 by Darrell

ABOUT THE AUTHOR

Darrell Schweitzer won the *Asimov's SF* Reader's Choice Award for the best poem of 2006 ("Remembering the Future," included in this volume), and has been nominated for the Rhysling Award twice. As a prose writer he has been nominated for the World Fantasy Award three times, once for best novella and twice for Best Collection. As an editor, he won, in 1992, for co-editing the legendary fantasy magazine *Weird Tales.* His novels include *The Mask of the Sorcerer*, *The Shattered Goddess*, and *The White Isle.* His short story collections include *Tom O'Bedlam's Night Out*, *Transients*, *Nightscapes*, *The Great World and the Small*, *Refugees from an Imaginary Country*, and *Necromancies and Netherworlds* (with Jason Van Hollander). He is also a widely published interviewer, essayist, and critic, whose credits range from *Publishers Weekly* and *The Washington Post* to *The New York Review of Science Fiction.*

www.ingramcontent.com/pod-product-compliance
Lightning Source LLC
LaVergne TN
LVHW011207080426
835508LV00007B/656

* 9 7 8 1 4 3 4 4 8 2 0 4 4 *